A GRAIL SIMPLIFIED COUNCIL
DOCUMENT

THIS IS
THE
LITURGY

THIS IS THE LITURGY

Simplifications of the
'Constitution on the Sacred Liturgy'
and 'Dogmatic Constitution on
Divine Revelation'

Benziger Brothers
New York
1967

Nihil Obstat: R. D. Richardus Stewart, S.T.L.
censor deputatus.
Imprimatur: ✠ Cyrillus
Archiepiscopus Southwarcensis.
die 19a Junii 1967

The Nihil Obstat and Imprimatur are official
declarations that a book or pamphlet is free
from doctrinal or moral error. No implication
is contained therein that those who have
granted the Nihil Obstat or Imprimatur agree
with the contents, opinions, or statements
expressed.

This is the Liturgy: Simplifications of the
'Constitution on the Sacred Liturgy' and
'Dogmatic Constitution on Divine Revelation'

Set in 10–11pt. Times
Made and printed in Great Britain

INTRODUCTORY NOTE

The Grail Simplified Council Documents
have been prepared by a Grail team
as part of the work to spread the teaching of Vatican II.
In the words of the
Decree on the Church in the World Today,
they are meant to assist the people of God
'to penetrate the world with a Christian spirit,
and to be witnesses of Christ
in all things in the midst of human society'.

To stress the biblical nature of the documents,
and to encourage the reader
to get acquainted with the sources,
scripture references have been included.

The discussion questions at the end of the book
have been devised to bring out the fundamental points
contained in each chapter of the documents
and to help the reader grasp their implications.

Philippa Craig.

TABLE OF CONTENTS

Introductory note

I CONSTITUTION ON THE SACRED LITURGY

Introduction

Chapter 1   **General principles for restoration**
Nature of the liturgy; its importance
in the Church's life   11
Promoting liturgical formation and
participation   15
Reform of the liturgy   17
I GENERAL PRINCIPLES   18
*II PRINCIPLES DRAWN FROM
THE NATURE OF THE LITURGY*   19
*III PRINCIPLES BASED ON THE
PASTORAL NATURE OF THE
LITURGY*   21
*IV PRINCIPLES OF ADAPTATION
TO NATIONAL CULTURES AND
TRADITIONS*   23
Promotion of liturgical life in diocese
and parish   24
Promotion of pastoral-liturgical action   25

Chapter 2   **The mystery of the Eucharist**   26

Chapter 3   **Sacraments and sacramentals**   29

Chapter 4   **The divine office**   35

Chapter 5   **The liturgical year**   39

Chapter 6	Sacred music	43
Chapter 7	Sacred arts and furnishings	45
Appendix	Revision of calendar	48

II DOGMATIC CONSTITUTION ON DIVINE REVELATION

	Introduction	
Chapter 1	Revelation itself	
	The Old Testament	52
	The New Testament	53
Chapter 2	Handing on divine revelation	54
Chapter 3	The inspiration and interpretation of scripture	59
Chapter 4	The Old Testament	61
Chapter 5	The New Testament	63
Chapter 6	The scriptures in the Church's life	66
Appendix	Discussion questions	71

INTRODUCTION

1 The purpose of the Council
is to renew Christian life,
to adapt Church institutions where necessary,
to encourage everything that leads
to Christian unity
and that helps to bring all men
into the family of the Church.
Therefore
the Council sees compelling reasons
for reforming and cherishing the liturgy.

2 For it is through the liturgy,
particularly the Mass,
that the faithful can express
in their own lives
and show other people
the mystery of Christ
and what his Church really is.
It is basic to the Church
to be at once human and divine,
visible and invisible,
active and contemplative,
present in the world
and yet a stranger in it.
The Church is all this in such a way
that the human is directed to the divine,
the visible to the invisible,
action to contemplation,
this world of time to the heavenly city.   (*Cf. Hebrews 13:14*)
Day by day
while the liturgy builds up the faithful
into a temple of God
into a dwelling place of the Spirit   (*Cf. Ephesians 2:21–2*)
in the likeness of Christ,
at the same time
it gives them strength to preach Christ.
Thus the liturgy shows the Church

to the world as a standard
under which all men may be saved.

3 So the Council states the principles
of liturgical reform
and their practical application.

Some of these principles apply
to all the rites
within the Catholic Church.
But the practical applications
concern the Roman rite alone.

4 Finally
the Church recognizes that all its different rites
have the same dignity and value.
It wants to guard and cherish these rites
and, where necessity demands,
to revise them
and to strengthen them
to meet the needs of today.

Chapter 1

GENERAL PRINCIPLES FOR RESTORATION

Nature of the liturgy; its importance in the Church's life

5 God 'desires all men to be saved',   (*1 Timothy 2:4*)
so when the time came
he sent us his Son the Mediator
whose human nature was the means of our salvation.
In Christ
mankind was reconciled with God
and from this reconciliation
we were given the perfect act of worship.

All that God did in the Old Testament
culminated in the work of Christ
who glorified the Father by redeeming us.
It was chiefly by his passion,
his resurrection and his ascension
that Christ achieved his task.
'By dying he destroyed our death,
by rising he restored our life.'   (*Easter Preface*)
And from this sacrificial death
the Church was born,
the wondrous sacrament.

6 Just as he had been sent by the Father,
so Christ sent his apostles,
filled with his Spirit.
It was their mission to proclaim
that by his death and resurrection
Christ had achieved our salvation.
It was also their mission
to extend the salvation they preached
by means of the Mass and the sacraments
round which the liturgy revolves.
So by baptism we are drawn
into the paschal mystery,
dying with Christ, being buried with Christ,
rising with Christ,   (*Cf. Romans 6:4*)

being adopted as God's children
and becoming his true worshippers.
Similarly, through the Eucharist
we proclaim Christ's death
until his second coming.   (*Cf. 1 Corinthians 11:26*)
Therefore
ever since the first Pentecost
those who receive Christ's word
have been baptized   (*Cf. Acts 2:41*)
and never cease to celebrate the Eucharist.
The Church has always come together
to celebrate the paschal mystery
by reading scripture,
by sharing in the Eucharist,
thanking God,
through Christ
and in the power of the Spirit,
for the gift he has given us.

7 To carry on this work
Christ is always present in the Church,
especially in the actions of the liturgy.
He is present in the Mass,
both in the person of the priest
and in the consecrated bread and wine.
He is present by his power
in the sacraments.
Therefore
when a man baptizes
it is Christ who does it;
when the scriptures are read in church
it is Christ who speaks
for he is present in his word.
When the Church prays and sings together
Christ is present among them
as he promised.   (*Cf. Matthew 18:20*)

The liturgy gives God supreme glory
and makes men holy
and in this great work

Christ always links the Church with himself.
It is through Christ that the Church
worships the Father.

In the liturgy therefore
Christ's priestly work is prolonged.
In the liturgy
the sacraments
together with many other visible signs
make us holy.
God is worshipped
by Christ together with ourselves.

In the light of all that
we can do nothing more sacred
than to celebrate the liturgy
since it is the action of Christ
and of his body, the Church.

8 The liturgy is a foretaste
of the way we shall worship God
when we reach the heaven
to which we are journeying.
In the liturgy
we call on the angels and saints
to join us in God's praise
and we look forward to Christ's second coming
when we shall share his glory.

(*Cf. Philippians 3:20; Colossians 3:4*)

9 The liturgy does not exhaust
the activity of the Church.
Before liturgy
comes the call to faith
and conversion of heart.

The Church's mission
is to bring unbelievers
the news of salvation,
to help them to repentance.   (*Cf. Acts 2:38*)
But equally its mission is to believers.

13

They must be prepared for the sacraments,
must be taught
and urged to Christian love and the apostolate.
Christ's followers therefore
must be the light of the world
and must let men see them
giving glory to God.

10 Nevertheless,
the liturgy remains the highest peak
of the Church's activity,
the well-spring of its power.
For the goal of the apostolate
is that all who are baptized and believe
should assemble to praise God
to share in the sacrifice
and to eat the Lord's supper.

In its own turn
the liturgy inspires the faithful
as they receive the sacraments
to share in the one holiness.
It prays that their manner of life
will tally with what they believe;
it renews the covenant between God and man;
it draws the faithful within God's love.
It is from the liturgy,
especially from the Eucharist,
that God is glorified,
that men are most powerfully sanctified in Christ,
that God's life comes to us.

11 For the liturgy to have its full effect
the faithful must come to it
with sincerity and awareness,
co-operating with this gift of God's life
so that it becomes fruitful in them.
Therefore
priests should realize
that liturgical celebration demands more

than mere obedience to rubrics and laws.
It is for them to ensure
that the faithful take a truly active part,
with awareness of what they are doing,
with spiritual benefit to themselves.

12 The spiritual life involves more
than taking part in the liturgy.
Christians must not only pray collectively
but personally as well
and our prayer should be continuous.
Christians must always bear in themselves
the dying of Jesus
so that the life of Jesus
may be shown in them too.   (*Cf. 2 Corinthians 4:10–11*)
That is why at Mass
we ask God to accept
our spiritual sacrifice
and to work on us until we too
become an eternal offering to him.
                    (*Cf. Secret, Pentecost Monday*)

13 The Council approves of popular devotions
so long as they accord
with the letter and spirit of Catholicism;
and if they result
from directives from Rome
or from local bishops.

Nevertheless
such devotions must be in keeping
with the liturgical seasons,
springing from the liturgy,
leading back to the liturgy.
There can be no comparison
between popular devotions and the liturgy.

Promoting liturgical formation and participation
14 The Church wants the faithful
to take part in the liturgy
fully, actively, deliberately.

The nature of the liturgy demands this;
and it is also the right and duty of Christians
arising from their baptism.

In any discussion of liturgical renewal
this consideration must come first.
Priests should strive
to bring about this participation
by every means in their power.

It is obvious that this will never succeed
unless they themselves are first filled
with the spirit and power of the liturgy.
Priests themselves
need liturgical instruction.
Therefore the Council lays down the following:

15 Those who teach liturgy
in seminaries, religious houses
and theological faculties
must be properly trained for this work
in specialized centres.

16 In seminaries and religious houses of studies
liturgy must be considered
a major and compulsory course of study,
and in theological faculties
it must rank among the main courses of study.
Other professors,
especially teachers of theology and scripture,
should show how the mystery of Christ
and the history of salvation
link up with the liturgy,
and they should make clear the unity
underlying all priestly formation.

17 In seminaries and religious houses
students must receive
proper liturgical formation
in their spiritual life.
They need this in order to understand the rites

and to participate fully.
They should take part
not only in liturgical celebrations
but also in popular devotions
which are liturgical in spirit.
Indeed the life in such centres
must be thoroughly imbued by the liturgy.

18 Secular and religious priests
who work directly with the laity
must be helped to an ever deeper understanding
of what they do in the liturgy.
They must be helped to live the liturgical life
and to share it with their people.

19 Priests must show enthusiasm and patience
in helping people to understand the liturgy
and to take part in it.
At the same time they should remember
people's varying capacities.
By doing this, they will fulfil
one of the priest's primary duties,
and they must lead in this matter
by both word and example.

20 Sound radio and television transmissions
of liturgical rites,
especially of the Mass,
must be done with dignity
and under the direction of someone
appointed by the bishops.

Reform of the liturgy
21 It is for the benefit of Christians
that the Church wishes to reform the liturgy.
What is divinely instituted in the liturgy
cannot be changed.
But what is not divinely instituted
can and should be changed when necessary.

The aim of this reform
is to ensure
that liturgical words and rites
express their meaning more clearly
so that Christians can understand and take part
as a community ought to take part.

To this end the Council lays down
the following principles:

I GENERAL PRINCIPLES

22 (i) The regulation of the liturgy
depends on the Pope's authority
and, as law decrees,
on the bishops'.

(ii) Within certain defined limits
it also comes within the authority
of local conferences of bishops.

(iii) Nobody else has any authority whatever
to add, remove or change
anything in the liturgy.

23 The revision of any part of the liturgy
demands historical, theological
and pastoral study,
and this should take into account
recent liturgical reforms
and current experiments.

This is necessary
if progress is to be made
and what is useful retained.
In addition
nothing new may be set in motion
unless the real good of the Church
demands it,

18

and as far as possible
new patterns should spring from existing ones.

Whenever possible
there should not be marked differences
between the rites used in neighbouring areas.

24 In celebrating the liturgy
scripture is vitally important,
for scripture provides the readings,
scripture is explained in the homily,
psalms are sung.
Collects, prayers and songs
are scripturally inspired.
Liturgical actions and signs
get their meaning from scripture.
So if liturgical renewal
is to achieve anything
then there must be encouragement
of that warm and vital love of scripture
which glows in the liturgy
of both East and West.

25 A revision of the liturgical books
is to be made as soon as possible.
Experts should make it
in consultation with certain bishops.

II PRINCIPLES DRAWN FROM THE NATURE OF THE LITURGY

26 Liturgical services
are not private affairs.
They belong to the whole Church,
that is, to the people with their bishops.
But they concern individual members
in different ways
according to the role they play
in the celebration.

27 Whenever the liturgy allows
for a celebration

19

in which the people take part,
this is always to be preferred
to a more or less private celebration.

This applies with particular force
to the Mass and the sacraments.

28 In liturgical celebrations,
all those who have a particular role,
priest or lay people,
should keep strictly to their own parts.

29 Altar servers, readers,
commentators and choir members
have a genuine liturgical role.
They should realize this and act accordingly.

Moreover, they should be given training
for their roles.

30 Congregations should be encouraged
to take part
by singing, by action,
by gesture, by bodily attitudes
and sometimes also
by reverent silence.

31 In the forthcoming revision
of the liturgical books
provision must be made
for the people to take part.

32 Certain distinctions
are made in the liturgy
according to liturgical functions
and according to clerical or civil rank,
but apart from this
no person or persons is to be given
any particular honours
or exceptional treatment.

33 Though the liturgy is first of all
the worship of God,
it is also instruction for the people
since God speaks to them in the liturgy
and they reply to him.

The prayers made to God
by the presiding priest
are said on behalf of all who are present,
and of the whole Church.
So when the Church prays, sings and acts,
this strengthens its people's faith
and raises their minds to God
that they may serve him better
and be more receptive to his gift of life.

Therefore
in revision of the liturgy
the following principles must be observed:

34 Liturgical rites should be short and clear,
noble and simple,
easy to understand
and needing little explanation.

35 Scripture readings should be more varied
and more suitable than the present ones.

This will help to show the link between
what is done and what is said
in the liturgy.

The sermon is part
of the liturgical service
so the rubrics should indicate
its best position in the service.
Priests should be faithful and exact

in their duty or preaching.
Their sermons,
based on scripture and liturgy,
should proclaim what God has done
in the history of salvation
or in the mystery of Christ.

Direct liturgical instruction
should be given to the people,
if need be at suitable moments
within the actual service.

Scripture services should be encouraged
for various occasions
in the liturgical year,
especially when no priest is available.
Then they should be taken by a deacon
or by someone authorized by the bishop.

36 (i) Latin is to be kept
    for the Latin rites
    though all existing exemptions
    remain in force.

  (ii) And since the use of their own language
    benefits the people,
    this may be extended
    in the Mass, the sacraments
    and the liturgy in general.
    This applies first of all
    to readings and directives
    and to certain prayers and chants.

 (iii) On this basis
    it is for local bishops' conferences
    to decide
    if and to what extent
    their own languages shall be used.
    Then the Pope will confirm their decisions.
    These conferences of bishops

may need to consult each other
when their people share a common language.

(iv) Vernacular texts
meant for liturgical use
must be approved
by local bishops' conferences.

IV PRINCIPLES OF ADAPTATION TO NATIONAL CULTURES AND TRADITIONS

37 The Church has no wish to impose
a uniform liturgy.
It prefers to encourage
the individuality
of different nations and peoples.
It admits elements of their cultures
and traditions
into the actual liturgy
provided they harmonize with it.

38 When liturgical books are revised,
scope must be left
for valid adaptation and differences,
provided these do not destroy
the basic unity of the Roman rite.
This applies particularly to mission lands.

39 It is for local bishops' conferences
to specify adaptations
in liturgical language,
in music and art,
in sacramentals;
and above all
in the giving of the sacraments.
Any adaptation must tally with
the basic principles of this document.

40 When more radical adaptations are needed
– and some places and circumstances demand it –

then the local bishops' conferences
must carefully consider
which elements from national life and culture
can be used in the liturgy.

Their suggestions should be submitted
for the consent of the Holy See
for a given experimental period
among certain peoples.

The adaptation of the liturgy,
especially in mission lands,
is no simple matter
and the work must be done by experts.

Promotion of liturgical life in diocese and parish
41 The bishop should be considered
as his people's high priest,
on whom, in some sense,
their spiritual lives depend.

Therefore all should value
the liturgical life of their diocese,
which centres round the bishop.
They should understand
that the Church is most clearly manifested
when all the faithful actively share
in the same liturgy and worship,
particularly in the Eucharist,
joining in the common prayer
under the presidency of their bishop.

42 Since he cannot always preside
over all his people
in his cathedral
the bishop must set up smaller groupings.
Of these the parish ranks first.
In some way the parish stands
for the whole Church made visible locally.

Therefore efforts should be made
by priests and people
to foster relations with the bishop,
to deepen parish liturgical life,
to strengthen a parish sense of community,
especially in the Mass on Sundays.

Promotion of pastoral-liturgical action
43 Eagerness to restore the liturgy
is truly inspired by the Spirit.
It is an outstanding mark of the Church today,
indeed of contemporary religious thought.

44 In the light of this fact
the Council rules
that local bishops' conferences
should set up commissions on liturgy,
church music and art
and on pastoral practice.
These commissions should be assisted
by experts, whether clerical or lay,
and possibly
by some sort of Institute of Pastoral Liturgy.
Guided by the bishops
the commissions should regulate
pastoral action in the area;
should promote study and experiment
and propose suitable adaptations
to the Holy See.

45 Similarly,
each bishop should set up and direct
a diocesan liturgical commission
unless it is more helpful
for several dioceses to join forces.

46 Each diocese should also, if possible,
set up commissions
for church music and art.

These must work so closely
that often they can best be combined
into one single commission.

Chapter 2

THE MYSTERY OF THE EUCHARIST

47 It was at the last supper
that Christ instituted the Eucharist.
He did this in order to extend the sacrifice
through the centuries
until the Lord returns.
He left the Church a memory
of his death and resurrection,
a sacrament of love and unity,
a paschal meal in which he is our food
and we are given life.

48 Therefore the Church wants the faithful
to come to this Communion
not as strangers
but taking part, lovingly and fully,
understanding the rites and the words,
realizing what we are doing.
Taught by God's word,
fed by Christ's Body,
we should thank God
by offering his Son,
not only at the priest's hands,
but ourselves with him
and through Christ, the Mediator,
become more closely united with God
and with one another.

49 In order to make the Mass,
even in its words and actions,
as helpful as possible to the people,
the Council makes the following decisions:

50 The Mass rite is to be revised
to make clear
its essential nature and purpose
and to make it easier for the people
to take part in it.

To this end
the rites are to be simplified,
additions of little value to be discarded
and elements which have been lost
to be restored,
as may seem useful or necessary.

51 At the Lord's table
the people are to hear more of God's word
by a fuller use of the Bible.

52 The homily uses the scriptures
to present the Christian life.
It is part of the liturgy
and as a rule it should be given
at public Masses on Sundays
and days of obligation.

53 On these days,
the Bidding Prayers should be restored,
prayers which intercede for the Church,
for the civil authorities,
for those in need
and for all mankind.

54 In these Masses
our own language may be used
in the readings from the Bible
and the Bidding Prayers
and also, depending on local conditions,
in those parts of the liturgy
which belong to the people.

At the same time
the people should also know
their parts of the Mass in Latin.

Provision is made in the Constitution
for wider use of the vernacular.

55 The Council urges the faithful
to take part more perfectly in the Mass
by receiving Holy Communion
at that same sacrifice.

The bishops may allow Communion
under the form of bread and wine
not only to priests and religious
but, in certain cases to be determined by Rome,
to lay people too.
For instance, to a newly baptized adult
at the Mass after his baptism.

56 The two parts of the Mass,
the service of the word of God
and the service of thanksgiving,
are so closely linked that they make up
one single act of worship.
Therefore the Council urges priests
to keep on teaching the people
to take their part in the whole Mass.

57 (i) Concelebration,
which proclaims the unity of the priesthood,
was retained in use in the Church
in both East and West.
The Council extends permission
for concelebration
to any Mass on Maundy Thursday,
to Masses during synods, courses
and bishops' conferences
and to the Mass for the blessing of an abbot.
Subject to the permission by the local bishop,

it may also take place
at the community Mass in religious houses,
at the principal Mass in churches,
at Mass celebrated at gatherings of priests.

(ii) It is for the bishops to make rulings
about concelebration in their dioceses.
Still, every priest keeps his right
to celebrate Mass individually
though not in the same church
at the same time
as a concelebrated Mass,
nor on Maundy Thursday.

58 A new rite for concelebration
is to be drawn up
and added to the missal.

Chapter 3

SACRAMENTS AND SACRAMENTALS

59 The sacraments exist
to make men holy,
to build up the body of Christ,
and to give worship to God.
As signs they also instruct men.
They deepen and express faith,
they have the power to give God's life.
Now this divine life is strengthened in men
by the way they themselves receive the sacraments.

So it is essential
that the faithful should thoroughly understand
these sacramental signs
and receive them frequently
for the development of their Christian lives.

60 In addition to sacraments
the Church has sacramentals;

symbols of spiritual effects to be obtained
through the Church's prayer.
Sacramentals help men
to receive the sacraments fittingly
and they sanctify various occasions in daily life.

61 Thus sacraments and sacramentals
sanctify almost all the events
of everyday life.
They give the faithful access
to the life that flows
from Christ's death and resurrection,
the source from which they draw their own power.
The use of all material things
can thus be directed
to praising God
and to sanctifying men.

62 Today the rites of sacraments
and sacramentals
need adaptation to current needs,
for in the course of time
their meaning has become obscure.
Therefore the Council decrees the following:

63 Since the faithful are helped
by hearing their own language,
this may be used in giving sacraments
and sacramentals,
according to what is laid down elsewhere
in this document.

Local conferences of bishops
should straightaway prepare
and submit for Rome's approval
rituals adapted to local needs,
including language needs.
These may then be introduced.
These new rituals must be in harmony
with the revised Roman ritual.

That book contains an introduction
to each rite,
either of pastoral instruction
or teaching about the rubrics
or the social importance of the rite.
These instructions must be retained
in any new local ritual.

64 The catechumenate for adults
is to be restored.
The instruction of would-be converts
is now to comprise several stages.
These may be marked by a series
of liturgical rites,
celebrated at intervals
during the catechumenate.

65 Certain elements of particular rites
found in mission countries
may allow for adaptation
to Christian purposes.
When this is the case,
they may be admitted to the liturgy
according to what is said in paragraphs 37 – 40
of this Document.

66 There should be revision
of both simple and solemn rites
of adult baptism,
the latter taking account
of the restored catechumenate.
A special baptism Mass is to be added
to the Roman Missal.

67 The rite for baptizing babies
should also be revised
and made appropriate.
The rite should also show more plainly
the godparents' rights and duties.

68 The baptismal rite must include variants
for certain occasions,
for instance,
when many are baptized together.
Further, a briefer rite should be composed as well,
for use by catechists
in developing countries,
or by lay people baptizing a person
who is in danger of death.

69 A new rite should also be drawn up
to replace the existing one
which follows on an emergency baptism.
This must show clearly and suitably
that the baby has already been received
into the Church.

Further, a new rite should be drawn up
for validly baptized converts,
indicating that they are now admitted
to the fullest communion with the Church.

70 Except at Easter time,
the water for baptizing
is to be blessed as part of the baptismal rite.

71 The rite of confirmation is to be revized
and is to show how this sacrament
is one of Christian initiation.
Therefore, people about to be confirmed
should renew their baptismal promises
immediately beforehand.

Confirmation may be given during Mass,
or, if not, the rite should be introduced
by a special formula.

72 The rule and formula
for the sacrament of penance
is to be revised

so as to show more clearly
what it is and what it does.

73 What used to be called
'extreme unction'
is better called 'anointing of the sick'.
This is not meant only for the dying
but for any of the faithful
beginning to be in danger of death
whether from sickness or old age.

74 A continuous rite for the sacrament
should be drawn up
in which the sick person confesses,
is anointed
and then receives Communion.

75 A sick person may be anointed
several times
according to circumstances.
Therefore the accompanying prayers
should be revised
to suit that person's condition.

76 There should be revision
of both ceremonies and texts
of the ordination of priests.
The bishop's address may be in our own language
at the ordination of priests
or the consecration of a bishop.
In the case of the latter,
the laying on of hands
done by all the bishops
may be done by all the bishops
who are present.

77 The present Roman rite of marriage
should be revised
to make clear to husband and wife
the divine life given by the sacrament
and the duties of each.

Suitable customs
and ceremonies already in use locally
should be kept.

Moreover, local bishops' conferences
can draw up their own rites
for local conditions,
subject to the approval of Rome.
Whatever the rite, it must always
ensure that the priest
asks for and obtains the consent
of the two partners.

78 Marriage should usually be celebrated
during Mass
after the gospel and sermon.
The prayer
at present said for the bride only
is to be revised
and may be said in our own language.
It should remind husband and wife
that they are both equally obliged
to fidelity.

When the marriage does not take place at Mass,
then the epistle and gospel
of the wedding Mass should be read,
and the bride and bridegroom
should always receive a blessing.

79 Sacramentals are to be revised
in accordance with existing principles
and with current needs.
The faithful can then take part
easily and intelligently.

In certain circumstances,
some sacramentals can well be given
by lay people.
This is at the bishops' discretion.

80 There should be revision of
the present Roman rite
for the consecration of virgins.

A new rite is to be created
for religious professions
and renewal of vows.
This should increase
the uniformity,
the sobriety, the dignity
of these occasions
and normally should take place during Mass.

81 Funeral rites should show more clearly
the link between a Christian's death
and Christ's resurrection and victory.
These rites should also consider various
different national traditions
concerning funerals
not excluding the liturgical colours
to be used on these occasions.

82 There should be revision
of the rite for the burial of young children
with a special Mass for the occasion.

Chapter 4

THE DIVINE OFFICE

83 Christ the priest
unites mankind with himself
in his praise of the Father,
for he continues his work through the Church
which never ceases to praise God
and to intercede for the world.
It does this chiefly through the Eucharist
but also by praying the divine office.

84 By ancient tradition,
all the hours of day and night
are made holy by praise given to God
in the divine office.
When this is prayed
it is truly the voice of the Church,
the Bride speaking to the Bridegroom,
and it is truly the prayer
which Christ and the members of his body
offer together to the Father.

85 Therefore all who say the office
are sharing in a duty and an honour,
for when they do so
they are spokesmen for the whole Church.

86 The divine office is essential
for priests doing pastoral work,
for St Paul said:
'Pray without ceasing'. *(1 Thessalonians 5:17)*
Without God they can do nothing
and their work will effect nothing. *(Cf. John 15:5)*
It was precisely to devote themselves
'to prayer and the ministry of the word' *(Acts 6:4)*
that the apostles established
deacons in the Church.

87 The Council wishes to extend
the reform of the office already begun
so that it can be prayed
more perfectly today.

88 Therefore it decrees
that the traditional sequence of the hours
is to be restored
and related to the relevant time of day,
so far as modern conditions allow.

89 In revision of the office,
the following principles must be observed:

Lauds or morning prayers
and Vespers or evening prayers
must be seen as chief hours of the office.

Compline is to be adapted to form a suitable prayer
for the end of the day.

Though Matins, when sung by a community
is a night prayer,
it shall be adapted for individual recitation
at any time.

The office of Prime
is no longer to be said.

Communities shall still sing
the hours of Terce, Sext and None
but individuals may select
any one of these three hours,
according to the time of day.

90 Because the divine office
is the Church's public prayer,
it helps those who say it
in their own personal prayer.
They should pray with their minds
as well as their voices.
To this end
they should deepen their study of the Bible,
particularly of the Psalms.

Those who revise the office
should set out to make it easier
and more beneficial
for those who say it.

91 The Psalms, which at present
are said during one week,
are to be spread over a longer period
and the revision of the Psalter,

37

already under way,
is to be finished as soon as possible.

92 Readings drawn from ecclesiastical writers
should be selected more carefully;
those drawn from lives of saints
should give fact and not legend.

93 Hymns used in the office
are to be pruned or changed
to make them more suitable
and it is legitimate to choose other hymns
as occasions arise.

94 To sanctify the day
it is best for the hours to be prayed
at the canonical times.

95 Canons regular, monks, nuns
and others who must do so,
should pray the office in its entirety.

Cathedral or collegiate chaplains
must pray the particular hours they are bound to.

All members of any of these communities
who are deacons, priests,
or solemnly professed,
are bound to pray privately
any hours they did not pray in community.
This does not apply to lay brothers.

96 Subdeacons deacons and priests,
not bound to office in choir,
must still pray the whole office daily,
privately or together.

97 Nevertheless, bishops
may dispense their priests

from all or part of the office
or change it for something else.

98 Religious and others
who pray parts of the office
or a short form of prayer
based on the office
are also joining in the public prayer
of the Church.

99 Since the office is the public prayer
of the whole body of Christ,
priests not obliged to community recitation
are encouraged to pray
at least a part of it together.

The Council recommends
that the office be sung
when this is possible.

100 Parish priests should arrange
for Lauds and certain Vespers
to be prayed in common
on Sundays and feast days.
And the laity are encouraged
to pray the office,
either with the priests,
among themselves, or individually.

101 (i) Priests should use Latin for the office
though the bishop can allow
the use of an authorized translation.

  (ii) Superiors of major religious houses
can give their subjects
the same permission
even if the office is said in choir.

  (iii) If a priest prays a vernacular office
with a group of lay people
or religious,
he is fulfilling his obligation
provided he uses an authorized translation.

Chapter 5

THE LITURGICAL YEAR

102 Throughout the year
Christ's work of salvation is recalled
by the Church
on certain days.
His resurrection is celebrated
weekly on Sundays
and annually at Easter.

Throughout the year
the Church unfolds
the whole mystery of Christ —
from his incarnation to his ascension,
to Pentecost,
to the hope of his second coming.

Thus the Church shows its people
the wealth of Christ's power
and in some mysterious way
makes it available to them.

103 In the cycle of Christ's mysteries,
the Church gives special honour to Mary
who is inseparably involved
in his work of redemption.
In Mary
the Church sees its perfect model.

104 In this liturgical cycle
the Church also includes feast days
of martyrs and other saints.
In heaven they praise God
and they pray for us.
By honouring them
the Church proclaims
Christ's victory over death.
It offers the saints

as examples to the faithful;
it appeals to God
through the merits they won by their lives.

105 Throughout the liturgical year
the Church continues to form the faithful
through the practices
of prayer,
of penance,
of charitable works.

106 From the Church's earliest days
Sunday has been observed
as the feast of Christ's resurrection
and has been called 'the Lord's day'.
For on this day
the faithful come together
to hear God's word,
to join in the Eucharist,
to recall to mind
Christ's passion,
his resurrection and ascension
and to thank God for the new life
he has given them.
The Lord's day is the original feast day
of the Church
and should be kept
as a joyful day,
a day of freedom from work.
Sunday is the heart
of the whole liturgical year.

107 The liturgical year is to be revised,
both to preserve traditional customs
and to suit modern conditions.
Certain adaptations can be made
on account of local conditions.
This is subject to the approval
of the bishops' conferences.

108 The principal feasts of the year
are those which celebrate
the mysteries of our salvation:
these must always come first.

109 The time of Lent has two aspects:
it prepares for baptism or recalls baptism
and it stresses the spirit of penance.
These two aspects should be clarified
both in the liturgy itself
and through instruction.

The Council urges a wider use
of some of the baptismal elements
of the Lenten liturgy
at present lost sight of,
as well as a wider use
of the penitential elements.

The faithful must be taught
not only the social consequence of sin
but the real essence of penance,
which is hatred for sin
as an offence against God.

110 Lenten penance
should not only be outward and social
but interior and personal as well;
it should take forms
that are possible and relevant
to the times we live in.

The Lenten fast
should everywhere be observed
on Good Friday
and, when possible, it should extend
until Easter Sunday.

111 Though the Church honours the saints
and respects their images

42

and authentic relics,
still their feasts are less important
than ones which recall
the mysteries of Christ.
Further, the feasts of certain saints
are often more suitably observed
on a local scale.

Chapter 6

SACRED MUSIC

112 The Church's music is the greatest
of its arts
and forms an essential part of its liturgy.

The importance of music
in the worship of God
has been stressed in scripture,
                    (Cf. Ephesians 5:19; Colossians 3:16)
and by the fathers of the Church,
while recent popes have explained
its liturgical role more clearly.

The closer the link between music and liturgy
the more sacred the music,
for the Church approves of all true art forms
and welcomes them into its worship.

Since the purpose of sacred music
is to give glory to God
and to make men holy,
the Council makes the following decrees:

113 Mass, the sacraments, the office
are ennobled
when solemnly celebrated in song,
with everyone sharing actively.

The language to be used
should follow the directions laid down
in this document.

114 The Church's wealth of music
should be cherished
and choirs promoted,
especially in cathedrals.
Bishops and clergy must ensure
that all the faithful are able to join
in the sung liturgy.

115 In seminaries,
novitiates and houses of study,
in schools and institutions,
Church music should be taught
by properly trained teachers.

Where possible,
colleges of sacred music should be formed
and composers and singers
given a truly liturgical training.

116 Gregorian chant
is suitable for the Roman liturgy
and, other things being equal,
should take first place.

But this does not exclude
other kinds of music,
particularly polyphony,
provided it accords
with a true liturgical spirit.

117 Liturgical books of Gregorian chant should be re-edited
and made available in simplified editions.

118 The faithful should be encouraged to sing
during liturgical services
and popular devotions.

119 Local musical traditions are important
and should have their part
in liturgical worship.
This is particularly true
in mission territories.

Therefore musical training for missionaries
should equip them to encourage
the traditional music of their peoples.

120 Though the most suitable musical instrument
in the Latin Church
is the organ,
other instruments may be used
if they are appropriate
and help the people's prayer.

121 Christian composers
should realize their vocation.

It is for them to produce
truly sacred music,
and they should do this
not only for large choirs
but for small modest choirs
and for the people in the parish church.
The texts of such music
should be drawn chiefly from scripture
and from liturgical sources.

Chapter 7

SACRED ARTS AND FURNISHINGS

122 The fine arts
are among man's noblest works,
and this is particularly true
of genuinely religious art.
By their very nature,

the arts try to express
something of God's infinite beauty.
They raise our minds towards God
and so they give him praise.

The Church has always sought
– and still seeks –
the help of artists and craftsmen,
asking that their work for the Church
be truly beautiful and apt signs
and symbols of supernatural realities.

Progress in technique
has produced new materials, new styles
and the Church makes use of them.

123 The Church has never claimed
any one style of art as its own.
It has given scope to artists
of many periods,
of many styles,
and has thus amassed a treasure.
Contemporary styles of art
are to be given similar scope,
so long as they truly contribute
to the praise of God.

124 In church decoration,
in vestments,
any sort of church furnishings,
bishops should look for noble simplicity,
not for splendour.

When works of art are clearly unsuitable,
either because they are debased
or because they are trivial or mediocre,
the bishops should remove them.

And they should also see
that the designs for new churches

facilitate the celebration of the liturgy
and help the people to take part.

125 There should be moderation
in the number and positioning
of pictures and statues in churches.
Otherwise, it may give scandal
and encourage dubious devotions.

126 In judging works of art,
bishops should heed the opinions of experts,
and of their diocesan commissions of sacred art
and of their liturgical commissions.

And it is their duty to ensure
that valuable works of art
intended for God's praise
are not disposed of.

127 The bishop,
either personally or through a priest
with knowledge and love of art,
should encourage artists to make works
inspired by the spirit of the liturgy.

Where found useful, schools of sacred art
may be set up.

Artists who work for God's praise
should understand that, in some faint way,
they are copying God the Creator
and that the things they make
should be the means of bringing people
nearer to God.

128 In the near future
there is to be revision of the laws
that govern the use of material things
in liturgical worship –
such things as actual church buildings,

altars, tabernacles, statues, vestments.
These laws must be brought into harmony
with the reformed liturgy and its demands.

129 Clerical students should be taught
the history and development
of sacred art
and the principles it is based on.
As a result,
they should be able
to appreciate and preserve
existing works of art
and encourage contemporary artists.

130 Pontifical insignia and vestments
should be used only by bishops
or those with special jurisdiction.

Appendix

REVISION OF CALENDAR

The Council does not oppose
a fixed Easter,
provided that others whom it concerns,
notably the Eastern Churches,
agree upon it.

Nor does it oppose
a perpetual calendar
for civil use,
provided this respects a seven-day week
to include Sunday
and leaves intact as far as possible
the succession of weeks in the year.

DOGMATIC CONSTITUTION ON DIVINE REVELATION

Simplification 'De Divina Revelatione'

TEXT PREPARED BY F. M. BENNETT

INTRODUCTION

1 The Council takes as its guide
what St John wrote
about the living Word of God
whom the apostles saw and heard;
about whom they taught,
that we might be united with them
in fellowship with the Father
and his Son, Jesus Christ.
Following in the steps
of Trent and Vatican I,
this Council
wishes to teach the whole world
how God revealed himself,
and how that revelation is handed on
through the ages
so that all men may believe
and that their belief may kindle hope,
and hope engender love.

Chapter 1

REVELATION ITSELF

2 In his goodness and wisdom
God has revealed to us his secret purpose (*Cf. Ephesians 1:9*)
that, by Christ becoming man,
men may come to the Father
by the power of the Spirit
and may share in his divine nature.

(*Cf. Ephesians 2:18; 2 Peter 1:4*)
The invisible God,   (*Cf. Colossians 1:15; 1 Timothy 1:17*)
in his great love,
speaks to men as his friends.

(*Cf. Exodus 33:11; John 15:14–15*)
He lives among them   (*Cf. Baruch 3:38*)
that he may call them

into fellowship with himself.
Acts and words unite
to reveal God's plan to us.
The acts of God, in the story of salvation,
make clear to us the meaning of the words,
while the words tell the story of the acts,
and explain the mystery.
The deepest truth about God
and the salvation of man
is revealed to us in Christ
who is both the Mediator
and the Fulfilment of the revelation.

          (*Cf. John 14:6; Ephesians 1:9–19*)

The Old Testament
3 God, through the Word, creates all things,   (*Cf. John 1:3*)
and keeps them in existence.
In so doing he gives men
an enduring witness to himself.   (*Cf. Romans 1:19–20*)
From the beginning he showed himself
to our first parents
that he might open for them
the way of salvation.

After they fell, he stirred up in them
the hope of salvation
by promising redemption,   (*Cf. Genesis 3:15*)
watching constantly over mankind,
to give eternal life
to those who show their desire for salvation
by their zeal in doing what is right.   (*Cf. Romans 2:6–7*)
In his own good time he called Abraham
to build up a mighty nation from him.   (*Cf. Genesis 12:2*)
After the patriarchs he taught the people
through Moses and the prophets
to acknowledge him
as the only true and living God,
the Father who supplies every need,
the just Judge,
and to wait for the promised Saviour.

Thus through the centuries,
he prepared the way for the gospel.

The New Testament
4 After speaking through the prophets
in many different ways,
he finally spoke to men
in his Son,
sending him, the eternal Word,   (*Cf. Hebrews 1:1–2*)
to dwell among them,
to show them what God is really like.
So Jesus Christ became man among men,
that he, the Word, might declare the words of God
and complete the work of salvation
entrusted to him by his Father.   (*Cf. John 5:36; 17:4*)
Whoever sees Jesus, sees the Father also.   (*Cf. John 14:9*)
So by his presence, by his words and deeds,
by his signs and miracles
but above all by his death and resurrection
and finally by his gift of the Spirit of truth,
Jesus completed the revelation,
confirming that God is with us
to set us free from sin and death
and to raise us to eternal life.

This Christian revelation,
this new covenant,
will never pass away
before the return
of our Lord Jesus Christ.

                    (*Cf. 1 Timothy 6:14; Titus 2:13*)

5 To God who thus reveals himself
man must give the 'obedience of faith',   (*Romans 16:26*)
freely and completely offering himself to God
in the homage of his intellect and will,
readily accepting the truth
of the revelation granted to him.
The grace of God and the power of the Spirit
working within men's hearts

and turning them to God
enable them to make
this act of faith,
enlightening the mind
and giving joy and peace
in acceptance of the truth
and belief in it.
The gifts of the Holy Spirit
bring faith to perfection
and deepen men's understanding
of revelation.

6 Through divine revelation.
God has chosen to give men
knowledge about himself and his will
concerning their salvation.
These are blessings which would otherwise
lie completely beyond their grasp.

The First Vatican Council declared
that creation itself
provides human reason
with certain knowledge of God,   (*Cf. Romans 1:20*)
the beginning and end of all things,
but it is through revelation
that even in the present time
men have true and certain knowledge
of divine matters,
though these are not in themselves
beyond human reason.

Chapter 2

HANDING ON DIVINE REVELATION

7 God has preserved
his revelation from error,
the revelation of the salvation of all peoples,

as it is passed on
from generation to generation.
For this reason, Christ,
who is himself the fulness
of the revelation of God, *(Cf. 2 Corinthians 1:20)*
commissioned the apostles to teach the gospel
which had been foretold by the prophets
and is the source of all saving truth
and moral teaching, *(Cf. Matthew 28:20)*
proclaimed and fulfilled by Christ himself
so that men may have a share
in the gifts of God.
This commission was faithfully fulfilled,
first by the apostles themselves
in their preaching, in their example,
in the practices they learned
from Christ's words and actions,
from living with him
and from the guidance of the Holy Spirit,
under whose inspiration
they and other apostolic men,
wrote down the message of salvation.

To preserve this living gospel
in all its fulness in the Church,
the apostles left bishops as their successors,
passing on to them the authority
to teach in their own districts.
Holy tradition and holy scripture
together make a mirror in which the Church
throughout her earthly pilgrimage
looks at God
from whom she has received everything,
till the time she is finally brought
to see him face to face. *(Cf. 1 John 3:2)*

8 Thus the apostolic preaching,
expressed in a special way in scripture,
is to be preserved
by an unbroken succession of preachers
till the end of time.

For this reason the apostles,
in handing on the message they had themselves received,
warn the faithful
to hold fast to the traditions
which they have learned
by speech or by letter   (*Cf. 2 Thessalonians 2:15*)
and to fight in defence of the faith
which was given once for all.   (*Cf. Jude 3*)
Now this tradition
handed on by the apostles
contains everything necessary
for leading the people of God
to holiness of life and increase of faith,
so that the Church in its teaching,
in its life and worship,
passes on to all generations
all it is and all it believes.

Under the inspiration of the Holy Spirit
this apostolic tradition
develops in the Church
as understanding of the tradition deepens,
as believers contemplate and study its teaching,
treasuring it in their hearts,   (*Cf. Luke 2:19*)
as they experience its spiritual realities,
and as her bishops preach
the truth they have received
through episcopal succession.
As the centuries pass
the Church grows steadily
towards the fulness of divine truth
when the promises of God
will be completely fulfilled in her.

The Fathers of the Church bear witness
to this living tradition
which feeds the life and practice
of the Church
in its belief and prayer.
This tradition has enabled the Church

to define the full canon
of the sacred books
and to read them fruitfully
and with understanding.
Thus God, who spoke of old,
still communicates with the Church,
the Bride of his beloved Son.
And the Holy Spirit
through whom the living voice of the gospel
is heard in the Church
– and through the Church in the world –
leads believers into all truth
and makes the word of Christ dwell in them.

(Cf. Colossians 3:16)

9 Tradition and Scripture
are closely bound together.
They spring from the same source,
they unite and flow to the same goal.
For scripture is the word of God
written under the Spirit's inspiration,
while tradition takes the word of God
which Christ and the Spirit
entrusted to the apostles,
and hands it on unblemished
to the apostles' successors
so that, enlightened by the Spirit of truth,
they may preserve it faithfully,
as they expound and proclaim it.
It is not from scripture only
that the Church draws its certainty
of what is revealed.
So scripture and tradition
alike claim loyalty and reverence.

10 Tradition and scripture
are entrusted to the Church
as one deposit of the word of God;
so the people of God
united with their pastors

in holding fast to this deposit,
remain faithful to the apostles' teaching
in Christian fellowship,
in the breaking of bread
and in prayers,   (*Cf. Acts 2:42*)
so pastors and flock are one
in the practice and profession of the faith.

The task of rightly interpreting God's word
both in scripture and tradition
rests with the teaching office of the Church
which is exercised in Christ's name.
This teaching office
is not above God's word
but serves it,
teaching only what has been handed on
by divine commission
and the help of the Spirit,
listening to it,
guarding it,
expounding it faithfully,
and drawing from the one deposit
everything that is to be accepted
as revealed by God.

So in God's plan,
tradition and scripture
and the Church's teaching authority
are so closely linked
that one cannot function without the others.
All together,
and each in its own way,
since they are all inspired by the one Spirit,
they are the channels of salvation to men.

Chapter 3

THE INSPIRATION AND INTERPRETATION OF SCRIPTURE

11 The divine truths revealed in scripture
have been written down
under the Spirit's inspiration.
The Church
relies on the belief of the apostles
and holds that all the books
of both Old and New Testaments
are sacred and canonical
because being written under the inspiration
of the Spirit,   (*Cf. 2 Timothy 3:16; 2 Peter 3:15–16*)
they have been committed to the Church
as the message of God himself.
God chose men to compose the sacred books,
using their abilities and powers
as he acted in and through them,
                    (*Cf. Hebrews 1:1; 2 Samuel 23:2*)
so that they wrote
only what is in agreement with his will.

Therefore
the message of the inspired authors
is the message of the Spirit
and the books of scripture teach clearly,
faithfully and without error
the truth God wished to commit to them
for the sake of our salvation.
Therefore,
all scripture is divinely inspired,
useful for teaching,
for refuting error,
for reforming men
and enabling them to live rightly,
so that the man of God
will be found complete,
ready for every good work.   (*Cf. 2 Timothy 3:16–17*)

12 However
since God speaks in scripture
through men and in human fashion,
the interpreter of scripture,
in order to see clearly
what God wanted to say to us,
must find out what the sacred writers intended
and what God wished to show us by their words.

In order to discover
what the writers meant to say,
the 'literary forms' they used must be noted.
For truth is expressed differently
in historical writings, in prophecy,
in poetry, and in other forms of speech.
The interpreter must find out
what the inspired writer intended
when he used contemporary literary forms
in the particular circumstances
of his own age and culture.
In order to understand correctly
what the writers wished to say,
attention must be paid
to the characteristic ways
of feeling, of speaking
and narrating of those times
and to the patterns men normally used
in their day to day dealings
with one another.

But since scripture
must be read and interpreted
in accord with the same Spirit
who inspired the writing of it,
attention must also be given
to the content and unity
of the whole of scripture,
its harmony with the living tradition
of the whole Church
and with the elements of the faith.

It is the task of scripture scholars
by following these rules
to penetrate more deeply
into the meaning of scripture
and into its explanation,
so that by such study
the Church's judgement may grow more mature.
Everything that has to do
with the interpretation of scripture
comes under the judgement of the Church
to whom God gave the task
of preserving and interpreting
God's word.

13 Although the truth and holiness of God
is preserved in scripture,
the wonderful graciousness of eternal Wisdom
is also seen
in the care with which he has adapted his words
to our understanding.
God's message is expressed in human terms
in the language of men,
just as the Word of the eternal Father,
having taken on the weakness of our flesh,
was made in every way like men.

Chapter 4

THE OLD TESTAMENT

14 In planning the salvation of mankind,
God, by a special dispensation,
chose for himself a people
to whom he would entrust his promises.
He made a covenant with Abraham   (*Cf. Genesis 15:18*)
and then through Moses with the people of Israel.
                                    (*Cf. Exodus 24:8*)

To this people
by his words and his actions
he made himself known
as the true and living God,
so they came to know
the ways of God with men.
When God spoke to them
by the mouth of the prophets
Israel came to a deeper understanding
of his ways
and made them more widely known
among the nations.   (*Cf. Psalms 21:28–9; 95: 1–3*)
The plan of salvation,
foretold by the inspired writers,
recounted and explained by them,
appears as the true word of God
in the books of the Old Testament.
All that was written
was written for our learning,
that through the steadfastness and encouragement
of the scriptures
we may have hope.   (*Cf. Romans 15:4*)

15 The purpose of the Old Testament covenant
was to prepare for the coming
of Christ the Redeemer
and for the messianic kingdom.
It did so by prophecy   (*Cf. Luke 24:44*)
and by showing its meaning
by various 'types' or pre-figurings.   (*Cf. 1 Corinthians 10:11*)
The books of the Old Testament,
in accordance with the state of mankind
before Christ brought salvation,
reveal to all
the knowledge of God and of man
and the way in which
the just and merciful God deals with men.
Though they are in part
incomplete and temporary,
these books show us God's way of teaching;

they give us a lively sense of God,
sound wisdom about human life
and a rich treasury of prayer.
The mystery of our salvation
lies hidden within them
and the Christian should receive them
with reverence.

16 God, the inspirer and author
of both Testaments,
wisely ordained
that the New should lie hidden in the Old
and the Old be made manifest in the New.
For though Christ made a new covenant
in his blood,   (*Cf. Luke 22:20; 1 Corinthians 11:25*)
still the books of the Old Testament are caught up
into the proclamation of the gospel,
and the fulness of their meaning
is revealed
in the light of the New Testament.   (*Cf. Matthew 5:17*)

Chapter 5

THE NEW TESTAMENT

17 The word of God,
the power of salvation,
for all who believe,   (*Cf. Romans 1:16*)
is set forth powerfully
in the writings of the New Testament.
When the fulness of time came   (*Cf. Galatians 4:4*)
the Word was made flesh
and dwelt among us
full of grace and truth.   (*Cf. John 1:14*)
Christ established the kingdom of God on earth,
revealing both his Father and himself
in his deeds and words.
He completed his work
by his death, resurrection and ascension

and by sending the Holy Spirit.
Having been lifted up from the earth
he draws all men to himself,   (*Cf. John 12:32*)
and he alone has the words of life.   (*Cf. John 6:68*)
This mystery which had not been revealed
to other generations,
was then revealed to his apostles
and prophets
in the Holy Spirit,   (*Cf. Ephesians 3:4–6*)
so that they might proclaim the gospel,
might kindle faith in Jesus Christ as Lord,
and gather together the Church.
The writings of the New Testament stand
as a lasting and God-given witness
of these things.

18 Everyone knows
that even among New Testament writings
the Gospels stand out supreme,
bearing witness as they do to the life and teaching
of the incarnate Word, our Saviour.

Always and everywhere
the Church still holds
as it always has held
that the four Gospels
are of apostolic origin.
The message preached by the apostles
at Christ's command,
they themselves and other apostolic men
later handed on to us in writing
guided by the Holy Spirit.
This is the foundation of faith,
the four-fold gospel
of Matthew, Mark, Luke and John.

19 The Church has held and still holds
firmly and consistently
that these four gospels are historical,
that they faithfully preserve

what Jesus really did and taught
while living among men
for their eternal salvation
till the day when he was taken up into heaven.

(Cf. Acts 1:1–2)

After Christ's ascension,
the apostles handed on to their hearers
what he had said and done;
they did this with clearer understanding
after they had been taught
by the glorious events of Christ's risen life,

(Cf. John 2:22; 12:16)

and by the light of the Spirit of truth.

(Cf. John 14:26; 16:13)

The inspired authors wrote the four gospels,
selecting out of the many things
preserved in oral tradition and in writing,
making some of them into a harmony,
explaining some of them to meet
the particular needs of their churches,
but always preserving the form of the proclamation
so that they told us
the real truth about Jesus.
They wrote with the intention
that either from their own memory
or the recollections of people
who had been eye-witnesses from the beginning
we might know the truth
through the teaching we have received.   *(Cf. Luke 1:2–4)*

20 In addition to the four gospels,
the canon of the New Testament includes
the letters of St Paul
and other apostolic writings
composed under the guidance
of the Spirit.
These writings,
according to the wisdom of God's plan,
confirm our knowledge about Christ the Lord.
They expound his teaching more fully,

they preach the saving power of his work,
the beginning of the Church;
they foretell its growth and glorious fulfilment.

For the Lord Jesus promised his apostles
that he would send them the Paraclete
to lead them into all truth.   (*Cf. John 16:13*)

Chapter 6

THE SCRIPTURES IN THE CHURCH'S LIFE

21 The Church has always reverenced the scriptures
just as it reverences
the Body of the Lord;
for from the table of God's word
and the table of Christ's Body,
it receives the bread of life
and offers it to the faithful,
especially in the liturgy.
As it has always done,
it continues to maintain the scriptures
along with tradition
as the supreme rule of faith,
since by the inspiration of God,
consigned once for all to writing,
they communicate without change
the word of God himself,
and make the voice of the Spirit resound
in the words
of the prophets and apostles.
So all preaching in the Church,
like the Christian religion itself,
must be nourished and regulated
by scripture.
For in these books
God the Father
meets his children lovingly
and speaks with them.

The force and power
in the word of God
is so strong
that it gives support and energy
to the Church;
is strength of faith for the faithful,
is food for the soul,
is the everlasting source of spiritual life.
Therefore,
these words are true of Scripture–
that the 'word of God
is living and active',   (*Hebrews 4:12*)
having power to build up,
and give a heritage among the sanctified.   (*Cf. Acts 20:32*)

22 Easy access to scripture
should be available
for all the faithful.
That is why from the beginning
the Church made its own
the ancient Greek translation
of the Old Testament,
known as the Septuagint.
It has always held in honour
other eastern and Latin versions,
especially the Latin Vulgate.
But since the word of God
should be accessible at all times,
the Church is concerned to authorize
suitable and correct translations to be made,
especially from the original texts.
And if,
when opportunity arises
and Church authorities approve,
these translations are produced
in co-operation with the separated brethren,
then all Christians will be able to use them.

23 Taught by the Holy Spirit,
the Church longs to deepen understanding

of the scriptures
so it may continue to feed its people
with the divine words.
Therefore it also encourages
the study of the Eastern and Western fathers
and of the sacred liturgies.
Catholic exegets and other students of theology
must join together
under the watchful care
of the teaching office of the Church
to use all available means
in their study and exposition of the scriptures
so that as many as possible
of those committed to the service of God's word
may be able to feed God's people on his word,
enlightening their minds,
strengthening their wills
and kindling their hearts with the love of God.
The Council encourages the faithful,
especially those devoted to biblical study,
to press on with the work so well begun
with zeal which is constantly renewed
in a task so dear to the Church.

24 Theology rests on the written word of God
and on tradition
as its permanent foundation.
Theology is strengthened and renewed
by contemplating, in the light of faith,
the truth contained in the mystery of Christ.
Scripture contains God's word;
indeed, being inspired, it *is* God's word.
Therefore the study of its pages
is the heart of the study of theology
as well as of the ministry of the word
or pastoral preaching,
of catechetics
and all Christian instruction
including, most important of all,
the liturgical homily.

25 In the light of all this,
clergy, especially priests, deacons and catechists
concerned with the ministry of the word,
need to read the scriptures constantly
and study them carefully
'lest they become
empty preachers of the word of God
who do not listen to it themselves';   (*St Augustine*)[1]
for they must share
with the faithful committed to them
the riches of the word of God,
especially in the liturgy.
The Council also urges all Christians,
especially religious communities,
to learn to know Jesus Christ
by frequent reading of the scriptures.
For 'to be ignorant of scripture
is to be ignorant of Christ'.   (*St Jerome*)[1]
They should eagerly acquaint themselves
with the text itself
either in the liturgy,
which is rich in scripture,
or by devotional reading
or by instruction
and through the other suitable aids
to be found everywhere today
through the encouragement of the Church's pastors.
They must remember that prayer should accompany
their reading of the scriptures
so that God and man may talk together
for 'we speak to him when we pray;
we hear him when we read the divine sayings'.

          (*St Ambrose*)[1]

It is the duty of the bishops
'who have the apostolic teaching'   (*St Irenaeus*)[1]
to instruct the faithful in the scriptures,

1 St Jerome, St Ambrose and St Augustine, together with St Gregory the
Great who is not mentioned here, are considered the four traditional doctors
of the Latin Church. St Irenaeus is one of the first great Catholic theologians
These famous early saints of the Church are quoted here because they aptly
illustrate the working of tradition in the Church.

especially in the New Testament,
and still more the Gospels,
by providing translations of the text,
with adequate explanations where necessary
so that the faithful
may become familiar with the scriptures
and imbued with their spirit.

Furthermore,
there should be editions of the scriptures
for the use of non-Christians.
These editions should have suitable footnotes
and should be judiciously distributed
by both clergy and laity.

26 So through reading and study
of the scriptures
may the word of God spread rapidly
and be glorified;   (*Cf. 2 Thessalonians 3:1*)
and may the treasure of the revelation
bequeathed to the Church
fill men's hearts even more fully.
Just as the life of the Church is strengthened
by the frequent celebration of the Eucharist,
so we may hope that the life of the Spirit
will in the same way be kindled afresh
by the growing reverence for God's word,
which endures for ever.   (*Cf. Isaiah 40:8; 1 Peter 1:23–5*)

APPENDIX

DISCUSSION
QUESTIONS

THE CONSTITUTION ON THE LITURGY

Chapter 1   General principles for restoration

1 In what ways is the Church *a)* 'human and divine'; *b)* 'visible and invisible'; *c)* active and contemplative'; *d)* 'in the world, and yet stranger in it' ?

2 Why is the liturgy 'the highest peak of the Church's activity' ?

3 If Christ achieved our salvation, why are his acts to be repeated in the liturgy ?

4 How have lay people been given a greater participation in the liturgy by the recent changes ?

5 How would you answer someone who said that recent changes at Mass gave them no time for their own private prayers ?

6 The Constitution stresses that an understanding of the nature and importance of the liturgy is essential. *a)* How can we help ourselves to understand ? *b)* How can priests help us ?

7 Why have some of the rites and practices from the liturgy of the early ages of the Church been revived and restored for use in the Church today ?

8 Why has the Church advocated and permitted the use of the vernacular in the liturgy ?

Chapter 2   The mystery of the Eucharist

1 The Eucharist is a paschal meal. Is this more difficult to realize in a large church with a large congregation ? If so, how could this be remedied ?

2 If the Eucharist is to unite us more closely with one another, must there be some social contact outside of Mass between members of a parish or community ?

3 Some people are reluctant to be lay readers. Suggest reasons for this. How could they be encouraged ?

4 Do you regard the sermon or homily as part of the liturgy ? Why does the Church say that the scriptures should be used in the homily ?

5 Some people complain of the distraction caused to them by having to change position constantly, to sit, to kneel, to stand. How would you answer them ?

6 What special purpose is there in concelebration at Mass?

7 What is the meaning of the Bidding Prayers? Why are they said at that particular part of the Mass?

Chapter 3   Sacraments and sacramentals

1 How can adults, who were baptized as infants, be helped to realize the significance of baptism in their lives?

2 Confirmation is being discussed, particularly whether it should be given at a later age than is now customary. What reasons are there for or against this change?

3 The revision of the rule and formula for the sacrament of penance will 'show more clearly what it is and what it does'. Draw up a definition of what the sacrament is and what it does.

4 Why is 'anointing of the sick' now used instead of 'extreme unction'?

5 For what reasons is it recommended that marriage should be celebrated during Mass?

6 Make a list of the sacramentals that you know. What is their place in the life of the Church?

7 Which prayers in the funeral rites do you think could be omitted to make room for others that would be more suitable?

Chapter 4   The Divine office

1 In what ways is the divine office 'the public prayer of the Church'?

2 How does the recitation of the divine office by religious and secular clergy benefit all God's people?

3 What is pastoral work? How does recitation of the divine office help a priest in his pastoral duties?

4 For what reasons are Lauds and Vespers 'the chief hours of the Office'?

5 How will a study of the scriptures lead to a more fruitful recitation of the divine office?

6 In what ways can the use of the vernacular be a help *a*) in public recitation of the office; *b*) in private recitation of the office?

7 Draw up a plan for using all or part of the divine office for the private prayer of a lay person for a week.

Chapter 5   The liturgical year

1 In what ways can each Sunday be said to be 'the Lord's day'?

2 In modern life it can be difficult to live in the spirit of the liturgy outside Church celebrations. Suggest some ways in which this could be done.

3 How is Mary 'inseparably involved in his (Christ's) work of redemption'?

4 What is meant by 'the social consequence of sin'? What forms of Lenten penance would be relevant to our times?

5 Why have some saints' feast days been excluded from the Church's calendar?

6 In what ways has the revision of the ceremonies of the Easter vigil made it more significant to those taking part?

Chapter 6   Sacred music

1 Priests often say it is difficult to get a congregation to sing. Suggest reasons for this.

2 What is the place and function of a choir?

3 Can music written for Latin words be successfully adapted to English translations?

4 How would you answer someone who said that the singing of hymns at Mass was a distraction from the prayers and actions of the Mass itself?

5 What factors would guide your choice of hymns suitable for singing at Mass?

6 'Christian composers should realize their vocation.' What is the vocation of a Christian composer?

7 Why is the organ the most suitable instrument to use in the Latin Church?

Chapter 7   Sacred art and furnishings

1 Would you say that recently built Catholic churches have made full use of new styles, materials and techniques?

2 How would you decide whether a feature in a church building truly contributed to the praise of God?

3 Some old churches cannot be adapted for the liturgical

75

changes, e.g. Mass facing the people, without their becoming less artistic, or even made ugly. Should they be left as they are?

4 List the things which an architect should bear in mind when building a church today.

5 If an artist is to be 'inspired by the spirit of the liturgy', what steps could he take to bring this about?

6 Some priests discuss with their parishioners the plans for a new church. What could be the advantages of this?

7 Would the laity benefit from some instruction in sacred art?

CONSTITUTION ON DIVINE REVELATION

Chapter 1   Revelation itself

1 What can we discover about God by looking at his creation?

2 Read John 5: 19–47 and list the ways in which Christ says that he shows us the Father.

3 If God has revealed his purpose for mankind, why are there many people who do not discover it?

4 What things would you include in 'a zeal for doing what is right' which God sees as a man's love for him?

5 We have to give to God 'the obedience of faith' and 'the homage of our intellect and will'. Does this mean that we have to make no effort in mind or will to discover and accept God's revelation?

6 Do the people of God whom you meet today show that they have that 'joy and peace in acceptance of the truth' that the Constitution mentions?

7 In his Epistle to the Romans, Chapter 1, St Paul says of some men that 'the more they called themselves philosophers, the more stupid they grew'. What does he mean? Why did they go wrong?

Chapter 2   Handing on divine revelation

1 How is Christ 'the fulness of the revelation of God' if the Holy Spirit is still guiding and teaching the Church?

2 What is tradition in the context of revelation?

3 Why do you think we have no revelation as yet of future things such as the end of the world and details of the life after death?

4 In what ways can priests and laity bring about a united practice and profession of their faith?

5 Can the word of God be preserved faithfully and yet speak to people of every age?

6 If the Church is growing steadily towards the fulness of truth as the centuries pass, how do you explain the great heresies that arose and persisted?

7 What steps can priests and laity take to ensure that they hand on to the next generation the tradition that leads to holiness and faith?

8 Think of the qualities of a good interpreter of a foreign language. Are some of these qualities the same as those needed by the teaching Church?

Chapter 3   The inspiration and interpretation of scripture

1 How can scripture be used for 'refuting error' and 're-forming men'?

2 The four gospels were written at different times, by different men, for different readers. Find out these differences. What do they all have in common?

3 How does the Church ensure that God's word in scripture is not interpreted wrongly?

4 Make a list of five books or pamphlets written to help one understand more clearly what the writers of scripture wished to say.

5 Take an incident recorded by all four evangelists, such as the miracle of the loaves and fishes. Note the differences in style and content. Matthew (14:13–21; Mark 6:30–34; Luke 9:10–17; John 6:1–13).

6 'The interpretation of scripture comes under the judgement of the Church.' How does the Church judge this interpretation?

7 Some people argue that a very modern translation of the Bible will date in generations to come. What is the value of such translations?

77

Chapter 4   The Old Testament

1 What is meant by saying that God chose a people 'by a special dispensation'?

2 What did God's people in the Old Testament learn about 'the ways of God with men'?

3 Read Psalm 134 and make a list of the things that the writer of the psalm has discovered about God.

4 In what ways was Moses a 'type' of Christ?

5 Christ used the prophets in explaining his life and work to the two disciples on the way to Emmaus. Read Isaiah, Chapter 52: 13-15 and Chapter 53, and note what it tells about the Messiah.

6 The Constitution calls the Old Testament books a 'rich treasury of prayer'. Read Solomon's prayer at the dedication of the Temple, I Kings 8:22-53. What parts of this prayer could we use today?

7 What is meant by saying that 'the books of the Old Testament are caught up into the proclamation of the gospel'?

Chapter 5   The New Testament

1 How does the kingdom of God which Christ founded differ from the kind of kingdom which God's people had expected the Messiah to establish?

2 Read Peter's address to the crowd on Pentecost day, Acts 2:14-36. Note how he makes a summary of the story of salvation.

3 What is meant by the statement that 'the four Gospels are of apostolic origin'?

4 What is there in the liturgy and customs of the Church to show us that the Gospels were always held in high esteem?

5 Some of the Epistles were written to a small group of Christians on a special occasion on some special topic. What is it that the Epistles can teach us today?

Chapter 6   The scriptures in the Church's life

1 In which ways does the Church offer God's people the scriptures and proclaim them?

2 When we listen to scripture being read it is often some-

thing we have already heard before. How can we help ourselves to benefit from it?

3 What qualities would you look for in choosing a translation of the Bible for use *a*) for your private reading; *b*) for liturgical services; *c*) for a school text-book?

4 Make a list of all the new translations into English of the Bible which have been made in the last 50 years.

5 Would you agree that the Old Testament is not suitable for teaching to young children?

6 In what ways could you make prayer accompany your reading of the scripture?